Debbie Duncan's books are a word in season, speaking directly into our anxious culture. She retells Bible stories through the lens of emotion, in a lively and accessible way. The brilliant, two-tiered approach means that both little ones and older children alike will come away with a greater grasp of their emotional and mental well-being.
Katharine Hill, *UK Director of Care for the Family*

Adults and children will find this series thought-provoking and encouraging in exploring how we deal with feelings. We often hide from negative emotions, so books that help children face them, talk and pray about them, are an invaluable resource to promote emotional well-being.
Sue Monckton-Rickett, *Chair of the Association of Christian Counsellors*

Despite the increased focus on mental well-being around us, we rarely consider the emotional challenges of characters in the Bible. And yet, their feelings and responses are so helpful for us as we navigate our own obstacles and opportunities. This series gives parents and adults the tools to dig deeper with children and young people, enabling them to relate and learn from the valuable truths and experiences found in these much loved stories. These books will build emotional resilience and strong faith – and are great fun to read. What's not to love?
Cathy Madavan, *Speaker, author, and Kyria Network board member*

Debbie Duncan's God Cares series brilliantly helps children understand the emotions of Bible characters while encouraging them to explore their own emotions in the face of similar situations. What is more, the books do it in a style that retains the excitement and adventure of the stories themselves.
The books also offer practical help to parents and carers as they engage with their children on this voyage of discovery.
Bob Hartman, *Author and performance storyteller*

According to Barnardo's one in ten children have a diagnosable mental health condition and many, while they are undiagnosed, are unhappy and anxious for many reasons in today's world. Early intervention is vital before their feelings become more problematic. Debbie's God Cares series offers a gentle in-road for parents and carers to encourage them to open up about what they are feeling and what is going on in their lives. Learning early on how much God loves them and cares for them can only be a positive. Seeing their own feelings in well-known Bible characters will show them that no matter what the circumstance, God always wins!
Karen Lennie, *Cognitive Behavioural Psychotherapist PG Dip BABCP Member (Accred)*

GOD CARES

WHEN I AM ANXIOUS

Moses and Other Stories

By Debbie Duncan

**CANDLE
BOOKS**

To Reuben – keep trusting God, as he knows the
journey you are taking.

Published by
Lion Hudson Limited
Wilkinson House, Jordan Hill Business Park
Banbury Road, Oxford OX2 8DR, England
www.lionhudson.com

ISBN 978 1 78128 376 9

First edition 2020

Acknowledgments
Cover illustration by Anita Belli

A catalogue record for this book is available from the British Library

Printed and bound in China, January 2020, LH54

CONTENTS

About the Series

"In raising healthy children, it's not enough to just focus on the physical aspect of health. To be truly healthy, a child's emotional health must be nurtured and strengthened. Developing a mental attitude of wellness is also essential. When we adopt an attitude of wellness, we take on a belief that being well is a natural, normal state."

Jane Sheppard, "A Wellness Approach for Children", *Aspire* **magazine, 9 June 2009**

The *God Cares* series is about providing parents with a biblical approach to discussing emotions and behaviour with their children to provide an attitude of wellness. Children of different ages and at different stages of their emotional development approach things differently, so this series works on two separate levels: **readers aimed at five- to seven-year-olds, and chapter books aimed at children aged eight and above.** Please note that children progress at different rates in terms of their reading ability and emotional development, so the age ranges are only a guide for parents and carers.

The Bible stories are retold reflecting on the emotions. Children are encouraged to discuss this and relate the stories to their own situations. Sections at the back provide a reflective space for children, and practical advice for parents and carers.

About the Author

Debbie Duncan, the author of *The Art of Daily Resilience* and *Brave*, is a nurse, a teacher, and the mother of four children. Debbie has considerable insight into what constitutes resilience and bravery: the ability to cope, to stay on course, and to bounce back. In her books she considers what is required for physical, mental, and spiritual durability, interweaving biblical teaching and prayers with personal anecdotes and sound advice. This she now applies specifically to support parents and carers raising children.

Introduction

Even though it was written a very long time ago, the Bible has many stories and parables in it that can help us make sense of the world we live in. That is because it is God's word. The Bible can also help us to understand how we are feeling and how we can cope with those feelings.

One such story is that of Moses, who became a great leader of the people of Israel many hundreds of years ago. He didn't always feel like a leader or know God would use him to help his people, who were slaves in Egypt. In fact Moses was quite an anxious man.

As the story unfolds, each chapter of this book also includes some other Bible stories to help us understand what Moses and others were going through, as well as some questions to think about and suggested activities.

We may not be asked to do something like Moses. However, we might find ourselves in a situation we are anxious about, or perhaps someone else is worried and that is affecting us. Worries are normal, but they can become too much. We can, however, talk to God about them and trust him. This is something that Moses tried to do.

Introduction

After reading the story, discuss it and how you feel with your parents or those who care for you. There are some talking points at the end of the book to help you.

CHAPTER ONE

LET'S MEET MOSES

Moses had an interesting start to life. He was born to a Hebrew family who were slaves in Egypt. His family and all previous generations as far back as anyone could remember had been slaves there. Moses and his people were also called the Israelites.

Instead of living how they wanted to, the Hebrew people had to work for the king of Egypt. The Egyptian people thought their king was a god – they called him Pharaoh, as it means god.

We are not sure who the pharaohs in the story of Moses were, but many historians think the first of them could have been called Rameses. He became a powerful pharaoh before Moses was born. He loved huge buildings and made the Hebrew slaves build many of them. He was so proud and arrogant that he made them carve his name on them!

If the people didn't work hard, they were whipped or even killed. Pharaoh was a cruel master. If you go to the country of Egypt today, you can see some of the buildings that were built during that time. The Israelite slaves may have built the pyramids. Many hundreds of slaves died working on the building sites, as everything had to be made by hand. There were no trucks to transport the heavy stones, and there were no diggers to dig for the sand that the workers used to make the bricks. Egypt was also a hot place so working conditions were tough. Despite the difficult times, the Israelites put their hope in God. He had always helped them in the past and so they kept praying for help.

Even though life was hard, God's people survived and did well. They prospered in the land of Egypt and Pharaoh didn't like it. He had also forgotten that, years before, a Hebrew slave named Joseph had helped Egypt to survive a terrible time of famine. Joseph's bravery and wisdom meant that the pharaoh of the time made him a ruler in the land. Joseph even married the daughter of one of the high priests, which was a huge honour.

Pharaoh was worried that his slaves would grow in number and one day plot to kill him. He loved being king and did not want anyone to destroy his kingdom. He commanded all the midwives that helped deliver the Hebrew baby boys to kill them when they were born. This was because he was worried these boys would grow up to be men who would fight him.

~~~~~~~~~~~~~~~~~~~~~~~~~~~~~~~~~~~~

In the New Testament story about Jesus' birth, King Herod was told by wise men that a special baby had been born. The wise men from the East had studied the stars and ancient writings, and knew there was a prophecy about the birth of a special king. They had followed an amazing star all the way from where they lived to Herod's palace in Jerusalem. They thought that this was where a king would be found and wanted to worship the new king of the Jews.

Herod ordered all his wise men to also study the ancient writings and scriptures. In the book of Micah they found a prophecy saying that the baby would be born in Bethlehem. Herod was a cruel king and was only worried about his kingdom. He secretly wanted to kill the baby and asked the wise men to come back and visit him after they had met the child. When the wise men had seen Jesus, God warned them in a dream not to visit Herod, so they headed home a different way. Herod then ordered his soldiers to kill all the baby boys in Bethlehem.

When people are worried, they sometimes do cruel things just to protect themselves and what they want rather than following God.

You can read the full story in Matthew 2.

Living in Egypt as a slave was a man called Amram. He was a priest in the temple and his role in his community was to serve God. Amram and his wife Jochebed already had a son and daughter. Jochebed then became pregnant and had a little baby boy. Not wanting Pharaoh to kill the baby, Jochebed hid him for three months. But then she realized she had to do something as he was getting bigger and probably making lots of noise. It must have been a worrying time. How do you tell a baby not to cry? The family must have been scared that any minute the baby would be heard and the soldiers would come. They had to trust God for the life of their baby.

So Jochebed found a large basket, probably used to carry or store things in, and coated it with tar to make it waterproof. She laid her baby in it and then hid the basket among the tall plants growing near the edge of Egypt's huge river, the Nile. In fact, some think it is the longest river in the world! Jochebed asked her daughter, Miriam, to watch from a distance. That was sensible as not only did she want to know what would happen to her baby, but also the Nile can be a dangerous place. It's up to 8 kilometres (5 miles) wide in places and up to

11 metres (36 feet) deep. Can you imagine how big the river looked, and how noisy and busy it would have seemed with people, animal, and boats? The Nile has over a hundred different fish that swim around in it, as well as snakes, hippos, and even crocodiles! Miriam must have been really worried about her brother. She did what her mother told her, trusting God would protect him.

The Egyptian people thought the Nile was a very special place because the area around it was rich with all sorts of edible plants. They also believed the Nile was a god. When Pharaoh's daughter went down to the riverbank to wash, she saw and heard the baby and probably believed the Nile had given him to her. The baby was crying, and she felt sorry for him. Miriam saw the princess and was very brave, as she stepped forward and asked if she wanted her to get a Hebrew slave lady to help with the baby. Miriam was very clever and fetched her mother. So, Moses – the name given to him by Pharaoh's daughter – was brought up by his own mother and sister, and the princess paid them to do so until he was old enough to live in the palace. Imagine Jochebed's amazement. Not only was her son safe but she was also being paid to care for him! Sometimes God answers our prayers in a way we don't expect. Jochebed and her family continued to trust God for Moses' future.

Moses is an Egyptian word that means "son". Pharaoh's daughter treated Moses as if he were her own son. That is how God treats us if we trust him. He is our Father and we can trust him. The Bible tells us that God created us, and if we trust him, we are adopted into his family. Moses is also a Hebrew word that means "to pull" or "draw out". Not only was Moses drawn out and rescued from the waters of the Nile, but later in his life he helped save more than 600,000 men, women, and children from drowning or being captured by Pharaoh's army when they crossed the Red Sea.

Try drawing something that shows
how you feel and tell God about it.

CHAPTER TWO

PALACE LIFE

Life in the palace would have been extraordinary for Moses. He was treated as a son of the princess and a prince of Egypt. He stayed at the palace and was educated by the Egyptians. He would never have been hungry or thirsty, and he would not have washed his own clothes, or cooked his own food. However, he may have attended the court like other members of the royal household and learned about making laws and ruling a great nation. Many of the royal family loved sports like archery and hunting. All these skills would have helped prepare Moses for his future role as leader of a nation. Moses may not have known that, but God knew what Moses would do in the future. Often God prepares us in advance for what might happen. It is only when we look back at things that we realize God was always there, helping us along our way.

Moses may not have known he was different from the other members of the palace. He would have shaved his face like the other men and worn dark eyeliner around his eyes. In contrast the Israelite men would have had bushy beards. Moses would have worn elaborate robes, bathed in water, and used scented oils to make himself smell nice. His life would have been very different from the slaves working in the palace or building outside under the hot sun.

Moses did not visit his own people until he was forty years old. We don't know why he didn't do anything until then. The Bible doesn't tell us how Moses found out he was different from the rest of the Egyptian court or why he did not try to find out about his birth family. Perhaps he had allowed the wonders of the palace to stop him thinking about his true home. We can do that too. We can be so focused on the wrong things that we don't do the right thing. We can also get so anxious about what is happening in our lives that we forget that God has promised us a new home in heaven if we trust him.

One of the best sermons ever preached was not in a church but to a crowd of people sitting on a mountain in Israel. Jesus taught them about what life is like when we trust God. He told the crowd that people who trust God are blessed as they have a place in heaven. In those days the people who listened to Jesus and followed him were putting their lives at risk because the Jewish leaders did not think he could possibly be God's Son.

Jesus told the people not to worry, but to seek God and what he has to offer. He told them not to seek power and riches like Pharaoh or Herod, and not to stockpile treasure on this Earth as we cannot take it with us when we die. He also told them that God knows the number of hairs on our heads and even knows every little sparrow.

Jesus said that worrying does not add more time to our life or sort out our problems. He told the people to look at the flowers in the field. They grow each day and do not worry like us. In the same way he cares for the birds and the flowers, God knows what we need each day to live. We can trust him as he made us and we are his children.

This great sermon can be found in Matthew 5–7.

~~~~~~~~~~~~~~~~~~~~~~~~~~~~~~~~~~~

One day, Moses went to visit his own people, the people he was really related to. He was shocked at how they were treated. He believed he could rescue them and that the Hebrew people would see him as their hero. After seeing an Egyptian beat a Hebrew slave, Moses went to the slave's defence and killed the Egyptian. He looked around and thought no one had seen what he had done.

The next day, Moses saw two slaves fighting and tried to intervene. He asked them, "Men, you are brothers; why do you want to hurt each other?"

The man who was mistreating the other pushed Moses away and asked him, "Who made you ruler and judge over us? Are you thinking of killing me as you killed the Egyptian?"

Moses was scared for his life. He knew that Pharaoh, his adopted grandfather, had issued a law stating that if anyone killed an Egyptian, they would also be killed. So, Moses fled from Egypt. He had found out that he was not a true Egyptian prince and that he should really be a Hebrew slave. Can you imagine how he felt?

Moses fled across the Red Sea and the desert to a place called Midian. There he met a wonderful family who trusted God. Moses married a woman called Zipporah and had two sons. He was able to learn from his father-in-law, Jethro, and his new family about the God of Israel rather than the Egyptian gods that the palace advisors had told him about. That is how Moses knew it was God speaking to him later in his story.

Moses worked for Jethro, looking after his sheep and goats. It was a very different lifestyle from the one in the palace. Time passed – Moses probably tried to forget about his past life and that he had killed a man, and even Pharaoh died in Egypt. God, however, did not forget Moses or the Israelite people, who were still crying out to him to be rescued.

There is probably a place you go to be by yourself. Next time you're there, talk to Jesus as he is with you. Sometimes we forget he is with us all the time. It's good to talk to him about what is going on in our lives. Jesus himself went up a mountain or out on a boat in the middle of a lake to have time where he could be quiet and talk to God.

CHAPTER THREE

THE BURNING BUSH

One day, while Moses was out in the hills with his sheep, he was stopped in his tracks by a strange sight. He saw a bush burning in the desert but there was no smoke and the bush looked as if it was not damaged by the fire. In the centre of the bush was an angel. God had used the bush to capture Moses' attention. Sometimes God uses the extraordinary to make us stop and listen to him.

Moses went to have a closer look. He heard God's voice and trembled where he stood, as God knew his name. God told Moses to take off his shoes as he was standing in a holy place. Moses would have known what it meant to bow or honour a king from his time living in the palace. We don't need to do that now when we go to church or visit holy places, but we should remember to show respect to our creator, God. That means we should sometimes sit quietly and let God speak to us. We should thank him in song and prayers for what he has done for us.

God told Moses that he had heard the prayers of his people, who were still slaves in Egypt. Then God told Moses that he was sending him to free his people. However, Moses didn't think, "That's amazing!" He wasn't thrilled that God was calling him to do something he had tried to do on his own forty years earlier. Moses didn't think he could do it – he was not as confident as he once had been. He didn't feel like an Egyptian prince anymore.

Moses was not someone you would choose to be a leader. He lacked charisma and confidence. He was an anxious man. Even when God reminded Moses that he would be with him, Moses was still worried about doing what God wanted him to do.

Moses asked God five times about the job he had given him. Firstly, he asked God, "Who am I that I should go to Pharaoh and bring the Israelites out of Egypt?" God reminded Moses he would be with him.

Then Moses said to God, "Suppose I go to the Israelites and say to them, 'The God of your fathers sent me to you,' and they ask me, 'What is his name?' Then what shall I tell them?"

God said to Moses, "I AM WHO I AM. This is what you are to say to the Israelites: 'I AM has sent me to you'". God reminded Moses of who he is, of his power and strength, but Moses was still anxious.

Moses didn't really know God and he was anxious that the Israelite people would challenge him. He was worried the people would not listen to him, but God told Moses the elders and leaders would listen to him.

Moses answered, "What if they do not believe me or listen to me and say, 'The Lord did not appear to you'?". God showed Moses his power by turning Moses' shepherd's stick into a snake and then changing the appearance of the skin on his hand, making it diseased and then healed. Can you imagine how Moses felt seeing this happen? Would he have been scared that his hand would stay diseased? God assured Moses that he could use these signs to show God's power.

Finally, Moses said to God, "I am not good at expressing myself and I can't speak out." Moses was worried that the people would not listen to him. He thought he would not say the right words, and that the Egyptians and his own people, the Israelites, would not listen to him. God challenged Moses by asking him who gives us the ability to speak in the first place?

Again, Moses asked God to send someone else. He must have been afraid and anxious about going to Egypt. In the end, God allowed Moses' brother Aaron to be his spokesperson and help Moses.

God answered each of Moses' questions. God reminded him that he is God by showing him miraculous signs and speaking words of truth. God knew how anxious and worried Moses was. Moses was scared to go back to Egypt – he felt like an outsider to the Egyptians and the Israelites, and was reminded of how he had failed the last time. God met each of Moses' anxieties by showing him his power, by being there, and by listening to what Moses had to say.

The Bible tells us the story of a man called Gideon. He was not a leader when we first read about him in the book of Judges. Gideon was a young man who had to learn to trust God like Moses did. He went on to become a military leader, judge, and prophet, and he led God's people.

In fact, when we first hear about Gideon, he was hiding in a wine press. In Gideon's time, a wine press was a large basin where grapes were pressed to make wine. He was hiding his crops from an invading army from Midian. An angel, who was God's messenger, appeared to Gideon, just like the angel appeared to Moses in the burning bush. The angel called Gideon a man of courage. The angel told Gideon he was going to save Israel from the invading Midianites.

At first Gideon did not believe the angel. Like Moses, Gideon asked God for proof that he was who he said he was. He asked for three signs to show that this would happen. God answered Gideon's request and Gideon went on to serve God and his country, saving Israel from the invaders. We don't need to ask God for signs. His words in the Bible help us to remember that he is with us.

You can read the full story in Judges 6.

~~~~~~

So, Moses headed back down the mountain and told his father-in-law, Jethro, what had happened. Moses' family were very supportive, as they believed God had spoken to him. Moses put his wife and sons on a donkey and headed off to Egypt with them. In his hand he held the staff that God had turned into a snake at the burning bush.

Have you ever felt that things were too difficult to do? What happened and how did you get through it? Having these feelings doesn't mean we have no faith or that we should feel we have failed. As we continue Moses' story, we'll see how God works in and through all these feelings and situations in the lives of the people in the Bible. He does the same in our lives today, too. Try writing down how you are feeling and then share what you have written with someone you trust.

This is a space for you to write in.

CHAPTER FOUR

THE GREAT ESCAPE

Moses' return to Egypt was very different to the time when he left it. Moses had to trust God that the people who wanted him dead all those years ago were not around anymore. God had promised Moses that he would be with him. God also warned Moses that although Pharaoh would see him perform many miracles, Pharaoh would not free the Hebrew slaves until the life of his son was threatened.

Not only did Moses have to show God he was willing to leave Midian, but God also tested Moses and his wife, Zipporah, during the journey. God wanted to know they trusted him, and would do as he asked.

As Moses journeyed toward Egypt, God spoke to Moses' brother Aaron. God prompted Aaron to leave Egypt and meet Moses and his family in the wilderness between the two lands. Although they had not seen each other for such a long time, Aaron kissed his brother. At last they could meet. At last God was going to use Moses to set his people free.

Moses still had many challenges in front of him. He had shown God that he trusted him, but he was still anxious about what would happen. Often, we know what we should do but we can still feel uncertain and anxious.

Before Peter, James, and John were Jesus' followers, they were fishermen. They owned two boats and were partners fishing the large lake of Galilee. They had met Jesus, and knew that he was an amazing teacher who performed miracles. Jesus had even healed Peter's mother-in-law.

One day, Jesus was standing by the lake of Galilee and the people crowded around him to hear him teach about a God who loved them. Jesus' words were life-changing and the people wanted to hear more. By the edge of the water were the two boats owned by Peter and his friends. They had been out fishing all night, but they had not caught much. They had just washed their nets, ready to put them away. The nets would have been heavy and tidying them up would have been tiring. Jesus stepped into Peter's boats and kept teaching the crowds. When he finished, he told Peter to head out to the deep water and let down his nets again.

Do you think this is something you would want to do if you had been out fishing all night and were ready to head home? Peter told Jesus they had worked all night and had little to show for it. He probably just wanted to go to bed, but Peter trusted Jesus. He encouraged the other fishermen to do as Jesus told them.

When we feel God wants us to do something, it can often cost us. We can be tired, but we know the right thing is to help someone in need. Maybe we just want to play with our friends, but we see someone who is lonely and know we should talk to them. Listening to God and doing the right thing can cost us something. Maybe we know what to do but are worried about what will happen. Moses had to trust God. Peter trusted Jesus too.

When Peter and his friends let their nets down into the sea, they caught so many fish that the nets started to break. The boats even started to sink because of the weight of the fish. People have worked out that the money they would have made from the two boats full of fish was the same as twenty-five years of wages for all the fishermen! Jesus asked Peter to trust him and follow him. Peter decided to do as Jesus asked. Jesus knew that if Peter, James, and John followed him, they would still need to care for their families. He helped them earn enough money so that they would not need to worry about them. Jesus showed Peter, James, and John that they could trust him.

You can read the full story in Luke 5: 1–11.

~~~~~~~~~~~~~~~~~~~~~~~~~~~~~~~~~~~~~~~

Moses and Aaron gathered all the leaders of Israel together and Aaron told them what God had told Moses. Moses must have been relieved that he did not have to speak to them. God did what he promised and allowed Aaron to be his spokesperson. Moses showed the leaders the signs that God had taught him, like turning his staff into a snake. The people believed him. They were also thrilled that God had heard their prayers. Their response to this news was to thank God.

After thanking God for his promise of freedom, Aaron and Moses headed to see the new pharaoh. What a scary journey that must have been! Moses would have been worried that someone might recognize him. He had to remind himself that God had told him that there was no one left that would want to kill him. He probably had to remind himself that God was with him.

When they met Pharaoh, Moses and Aaron told him what God had asked them to say. They announced that the God of Israel wanted his people set free so they could worship God and not be slaves. Pharaoh's response was something like, "Why should I do as your God says, as I do not know him?" Again, Moses and Aaron pleaded with Pharaoh to let the people go so they could head to the wilderness and have a festival there to worship God.

Pharaoh wasn't interested. He was more interested in the fact that Moses and Aaron wanted the people to stop work to hold their festival. In response, he made his slaves work harder making bricks. In fact, he ordered them to collect their own straw instead of supplying it to make bricks, so they had to work twice as hard. Some of the workers blamed Moses and Aaron that their lives were now harder than before. Can you imagine how Moses may have felt? He probably wondered what was happening, although God had warned him that Pharaoh would have a hard heart. Moses asked God, "Why has Pharaoh not changed his mind?" God reminded Moses of who he – God – was. He reminded Moses that he had heard his people's cry and was going to save them. Moses had to keep trusting God.

Moses and Aaron warned Pharaoh ten times before he changed his mind. Each time they warned that God would send a plague, a terrible situation to remind Pharaoh of God's power. Each plague was connected to the gods the Egyptians worshipped. God reminded them that he was more powerful than the Nile as he turned the water to blood. Their land became infected with insects, their livestock became ill, the people themselves developed nasty boils, there were thunderstorms of hail and fire, thousands of locusts ate their crops, and then terrible darkness fell upon the land of Egypt for three days. Each time, only the places where the Egyptian people lived were affected. The Hebrew areas were not harmed. Everything that God told Moses would happen, happened. Moses did not need to be concerned.

Finally God told the Israelites to mark their homes with blood so that their firstborn children would be safe. All the firstborn children in Egypt died on the final night, including Pharaoh's son. God reminded Pharaoh that he was not a god. This time it was not the Israelites mourning for their children, it was the Egyptians and even the royal household. The Egyptian people urged the Israelites to leave and even handed their gold and silver to them. Before it was daybreak, Pharaoh pleaded for Moses to lead the people out of Egypt. So, God led his people through the desert and toward the Red Sea.

At every point that God reminded Pharaoh he was stronger than his gods, he also reminded Moses he was with him. Anxious, worried Moses was able to stand before Pharaoh and do as God told him to. Pharaoh let the Hebrew slaves go after the tenth and most devastating plague hit Egypt and his firstborn son died. The Israelites survived as they listened to God and he protected their families. Moses led over 600,000 males and their families from slavery to freedom and the promise of a new home, just like God said he would.

You can read more about Moses in the book of Exodus in the Bible.

Why don't you sit for a minute and thank God for what he has done for you? Think of all the times he has helped you when you have been anxious. He cares for you and is interested in what you do and what you are worried about, even the things you may not think are important.

This is a space for you to write in.

CHAPTER FIVE

WHAT YOU CAN DO

The story of Moses is a helpful story as we are reminded that we can all feel anxious about things. Often these are things we have never done before, or perhaps we tried something in the past but failed at it. This is normal as most people can become anxious about things. Anxiety is a feeling that we can experience when we are worried, tense, or afraid about something that could happen in the future. One example is feeling anxious about moving into a new class at the end of the summer holidays or starting a new school.

There can be many reasons why we can feel anxious. One reason could be that we have experienced a difficult situation in the past and are reminded about it every time we are in a similar position. This is what happened to Moses. He murdered a man, thought he had got away with it and didn't, and fled for his life. He tried to forget about his past life. No wonder he didn't want to go back to Egypt.

Moses had failed when he tried to rescue the Israelites before. Sometimes when we fail, we don't want to try again as we are anxious that the same thing will happen again. One example could be failing a test and not wanting to repeat it. I failed my driving test several times and became more nervous each time I sat it. In the end I prayed and just asked God to take away my nerves. I knew I could drive as my driving instructor had told me I could do it.

Anxiety can make us feel tired. It affects our sleep, we can become grumpy, and we may want to eat too much or too little. Anxiety can affect our body. It can make us feel like our stomach is swirling around, or our heart is beating too fast. Some people feel sick or go to the toilet more often!

We can also become focused on the wrong things and those thoughts can take over everything. An example is someone who has been ill – they might be worried about getting ill again, and so they keep washing their hands so they don't catch any germs, and become super anxious that everything is clean around them. Sometimes our anxious thoughts become so strong that they leave us feeling tied up and confused. Try not to let that happen. Talk to someone you can trust.

Talking Points

The following questions are here to help you think about things. They are ideas for you to chat about with your parents, a teacher, someone at church, or another adult you trust.

Questions:

- Why was Moses' mother worried about him?
- What was the pharaoh that the older Moses had to talk to worried about? What could he have done differently?
- What do you think made Moses anxious?

- What do you think Moses was asking from God?
- What can you do if you feel anxious?
- What did God say to Moses to make him less worried?

God answered each of Moses' concerns. He also reminded Moses that he had a family that had cared for him as a baby. Aaron was going to go with Moses to meet Pharaoh.

The following list suggests a few things you can do when you are feeling anxious:

- Talk to people you trust.
- Talk to God. Trust God.
- If the same worries and fears cloud your mind a lot, then tell someone you can trust.
- Keep a journal and write things down. Share it with your parents.
- Write a list of all the things that you are thankful for.
- Make sure you are sleeping properly.
- Make sure you are eating and drinking properly.

Prayer

Here is a prayer you can pray. You may want to say your own prayer or write one down.

Dear God,

Thank you that you are interested in me.
You love me and want the best for me.
You made me and know everything about me.

You know all my thoughts from when I wake up until I go to sleep. Help me to trust you and talk to you, no matter how I feel.

I thank you that you are with me wherever I am.

I thank you for Jesus and that he died for me.

Amen

This is a space to write your prayers.

Remember:

- God cares for you even when you are feeling anxious.
- Anyone can feel anxious.
- There are lots of things you can do to help yourself feel better.
- You don't need to feel that you have to face things alone.
- You can always talk to God, family, and friends.

CHAPTER SIX

PRACTICAL HELP

for Parents, Carers, and Teachers

Written by Karen Lennie, Cognitive Behavioural Psychotherapist PG Dip BABCP Member (Accred)

According to psychiatrists Sadock, Sadock, and Ruiz, "anxiety is a diffuse, unpleasant, vague sense of apprehension". It comes from our mind's interpretation of possible and not actual dangers. Fear on the other hand is an emotional and physical response to a definite or known threat of harm. Fear and anxiety overlap but both can cause each other.

If anxiety begins suddenly for a child and the cause is not known, then it is good practice for them to have a medical check-up to eliminate any physical conditions that can mimic anxiety. Also check their diet as they may be drinking too much caffeine, which can be found in Cola, hot chocolate, and tea.

In the absence of a physical cause, reassure children that anxiety is normal at times and everyone experiences it. Being anxious can show us that we are alert and protect us, but sometimes our "alarm" goes off for a reason that is not dangerous to us. In most cases, the feelings will pass and go away, and, as long as they do not affect the child's daily life long-term, they should not be cause for concern. (Speak to your GP if your child is in distress for a longer period of time.) It can help a child, whose heart is racing, to compare it with a good exercise session. Usually anxiety is just a mixture of symptoms in our body and frightening thoughts.

Find out more about a child's anxiety. Ask how they overcame their feelings before you knew about it? What does their anxiety feel like? What makes their anxiety better or worse? Try to avoid giving reassurance that all will be fine. It may not always be the case and an anxious mind cannot process feeling fine. Instead, reassure a child that you are with them, and they will get better and learn to manage their feelings with the right help. Tell them that worrying is normal but that you will help them cope with it. Ask them to tell you more about their anxieties. Keep talking when they want to.

As a parent or carer, it is natural to want to fix everything for our children, but this can delay the development of their coping skills. Instead, support them as they talk and work through the things that make them anxious. The Bible does not promise us an easy life and is full of stories of people who cope with a range of emotions.

Here are some further suggestions:

- Acknowledge how a child is feeling and work with them on normal breathing and relaxation techniques, such as mindfulness and progressive muscular relaxation. These techniques are particularly helpful at night when childhood anxiety tends to be worse due to tiredness and possibly worry about the next day. You can also pray with a child, reminding them that God understands how they feel.
- Make sure a child knows the difference between a fact and a feeling. Never dismiss

their anxiety or any of their worries, for they are very real to them and we have the benefit of knowing that most of our fears and worries don't become reality.

- If a child can identify their anxious thoughts, try to have a counter-thought in place to talk back to their anxious brain. A good technique for children is to imagine the bravest person in the world is on a walkie-talkie with them and to consider how they would tackle what is wrong. Ask: Do you know anyone who handles this anxious feeling very well? How can you use what you know about this person and try it yourself? What would you tell a friend, who feels like you, to do?

- If a child's anxiety is specific to one area of their life, for example school, it would be useful to identify the behaviour of those children they mix with. Then consider, what else do they do with their spare time? Are they anxious when bored? What do they feel good about? What's good in their life?

- Encourage a child to be open and honest about what is going on in their life. Try to ask open questions. For example, rather than asking, "How was your day?" say, "Tell me about your day... what was the best part and the worst part, and who would make the worst/best teacher and why?"

- "Reverse psychology" is often helpful when talking to children, for example by asking, "What could I say that would not help you at all?" or "What could we do that would be a waste of time?"
- Keeping a simple diary is also helpful. Note what has made a child anxious on a particular day. Rate it 1–10, with 1 being the least anxious they have ever felt and 10 being the most anxious. That way, if they are faced with the same anxiety again, they can monitor whether they are coping better or worse, and why.

Often children's behaviour is their actual language. Their actions are often their words. A sore tummy can be anxiety, and a tantrum can be distress and not bad behaviour. What we say and what they hear are often very different. In a busy world it is difficult to have time for everything, but if we always listen to the small stuff, children are more likely to approach us with the bad stuff. Also remember there are some excellent resources – you are not alone. Choose one or two people that you feel you can talk to, and check with your child that they are happy for you to confide in those people about the situation. There is a large church family that will also want to help and support you.

Resources

The BRAVE interactive CBT programme:
http://www.brave-online.com/

Care for the Family – parent support:
https://www.careforthefamily.org.uk/family-
life/parent-support

National Health Service:
https://www.nhs.uk/conditions/stress-anxiety-
depression/anxiety-in-children/

Seattle Christian Counselling
(a US-based website):
https://seattlechristiancounseling.com/articles/
helping-your-child-overcome-anxiety

Young Minds resources:
https://youngminds.org.uk/

Other Titles in the Series

Readers:
Debbie Duncan, *God Cares When I am Afraid: Jesus Calms the Storm*
Debbie Duncan, *God Cares When I am Strong: Friends in the Fire*

Chapter Books:
Debbie Duncan, *God Cares When I Feel Down: Jonah and Other Stories*

Acknowledgments

I want to thank my husband Malcolm, Matthew and Eve, Benjamin and Ellie, Anna and Jacob, Riodhna, Rob and Emily – our family – for all their love and care while writing this series.

I also want to thank Anita Belli who is so gifted at illustration and captured what I was trying to say in the readers.

I also want to thank the Lion Hudson family: Suzanne Wilson-Higgins for that initial conversation, commissioning editor Deborah Lock for her patience, Jacqui Crawford for the design and layout, and Stella Caldwell and Eva Rojas for advice and poetry help on the readers (some of the lines are Eva's). You are just a few of the family!

Thank you.